ch

Tomás Rivera

Tomás Rivera

Jane Medina

Illustrated by
Edward Martinez

Green Light Readers
Harcourt, Inc.

Orlando   Austin   New York   San Diego   Toronto   London

Tomás Rivera was born in Texas.
He and his family went from farm
to farm picking crops.

Tomás helped pick crops all day.
It was hard work. But at night, he
had fun with his grandpa.

"Come quick, children!" Grandpa
called. "It's time for stories!"

"You tell the best stories!" Tomás said.
"I want to tell good stories, too."

"We can get lots of stories for you, Tomás,"
said Grandpa.
"Where?" asked Tomás.

"It's a surprise," Grandpa said with a wink. "Let's go now. Quick, hop in!"

"This is a library," said Grandpa.
"Look at all the books!" said Tomás.

"Read all you can, Tomás. It will help you think of many stories," said Grandpa.

Tomás read lots and lots of books.
He read about bugs, stars, and cars.

Soon, Tomás started thinking of stories all by himself.

Tomás started telling his stories.
Then he started writing them.

When he grew up, Tomás became a
teacher. He still kept writing stories.

Tomás Rivera's stories tell about
people picking crops.

Lots of people read his books.
They like his stories a lot.

Now his name is on a big library.
Many people visit the library. They go
there for books—just like Tomás did.

Think About It

1. What did Grandpa do at night?

2. Why did Tomás want to tell his own stories?

3. How did Tomás learn to tell stories?

4. Why do you think Tomás wrote stories about people picking crops?

5. What kinds of books do you look for at the library?

Your Own Family Story

WHAT YOU'LL NEED

 paper

 crayons or markers

1. Ask an older family member to tell you a story about someone in your family.
2. Write a sentence or two telling what you learned about that person.
3. Draw a picture to go with your story. Share your story with your family!

My great grandpa was a cowboy. He worked on a big ranch.

Good Crops

What makes plants grow into good crops? Make a poster showing what plants need so they can grow.

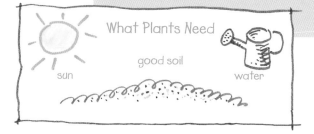

What Plants Need

good soil

sun

water

Helping Others

Tomás's grandpa took him to the library so Tomás could read lots of books—and learn to tell his own stories. Think of a time that a family member, friend, or teacher did something nice for you. Then tell your story to a friend!

Meet the Author and Illustrator

Jane Medina read a lot about Tomás Rivera so she could write this story about him. She hopes her story will help you think as Tomás Rivera did. If you work hard and do well in school, you can do anything you want to!

Edward Martinez had to find a lot of information about Tomás Rivera before he started painting. First, he found out that Mr. Rivera was born in 1935. Then he got photographs of people, trucks, and clothing from that time. He looked at the photographs as he painted. Do you think his pictures look real?

Requests for permission to make copies of any part of the work should be mailed to
the following address: Permissions Department, Harcourt, Inc., 6277 Sea Harbor Drive,
Orlando, Florida 32887-6777.

www.HarcourtBooks.com

First Green Light Readers edition 2004
Green Light Readers is a trademark of Harcourt, Inc., registered in the United States of America
and/or other jurisdictions.

Library of Congress Cataloging-in-Publication Data
Medina, Jane.
Tomás Rivera/Jane Medina; illustrated by Edward Martinez.
p. cm.
"Green Light Reader."
Summary: As a young Mexican American boy in a migrant worker family in Texas, future author
Tomás Rivera enjoys going to the library and listening to his grandfather's stories.
1. Rivera, Tomás, 1935– —Juvenile literature. 2. Authors, American—20th century—Biography—
Juvenile literature. 3. Mexican American authors—Biography—Juvenile literature.
[1. Rivera, Tomás, 1935– —Childhood and youth. 2. Authors, American.
3. Mexican Americans Biography.] I. Martinez, Edward, ill. II. Title. III. Series.
PQ7079.2.R5Z74 2003
863'.64—dc22   2003017482
ISBN 0-15-205146-5
ISBN 0-15-205145-7 pb

A C E G H F D B
A C E G H F D B (pb)

Ages 5–7
Grades: 1–2
Guided Reading Level: I–J
Reading Recovery Level: 16

Green Light Readers
For the reader who's ready to GO!

"A must-have for any family with a beginning reader."—*Boston Sunday Herald*

"You can't go wrong with adding several copies of these terrific books to your beginning-to-read collection."—*School Library Journal*

"A winner for the beginner."—*Booklist*

Five Tips to Help Your Child Become a Great Reader

1. Get involved. Reading aloud to and with your child is just as important as encouraging your child to read independently.

2. Be curious. Ask questions about what your child is reading.

3. Make reading fun. Allow your child to pick books on subjects that interest her or him.

4. Words are everywhere—not just in books. Practice reading signs, packages, and cereal boxes with your child.

5. Set a good example. Make sure your child sees YOU reading.

Why Green Light Readers Is the Best Series for Your New Reader

● Created exclusively for beginning readers by some of the biggest and brightest names in children's books

● Reinforces the reading skills your child is learning in school

● Encourages children to read—and finish—books by themselves

● Offers extra enrichment through fun, age-appropriate activities unique to each story

● Incorporates characteristics of the Reading Recovery program used by educators

● Developed with Harcourt School Publishers and credentialed educational consultants

Look for more Green Light Readers wherever books are sold!